A Simpler Path

Via

Julian of Norwich and Marcus Aurelius

By

David Conduct

Copyright © 2021 David Conduct

ISBN: 978-1-916981-83-6

All rights reserved, including the right to reproduce this book, or portions thereof in any form. No part of this text may be reproduced, transmitted, downloaded, decompiled, reverse engineered, or stored, in any form or introduced into any information storage and retrieval system, in any form or by any means, whether electronic or mechanical without the express written permission of the author.

Also by this Author

*The Great War: Lost and found

*All You Need is Love ~ A Julian of Norwich Handbook

*Rock 'n' Roll Years ~ Journal Reflections 1973 – 1998

*Essays on a Liberal Education

*The Holy Contour of Life ~ A Spiritual Journey

*A Word to Planet Earth

*Kindness and the Individual ~ An Introduction to

Vasily Grossman's 'Life and Fate'

*Mending a Broken Universe

*A Gardener for Man ~ An Introduction to William

Langland's 'Vision of Piers Plowman'

*Dramatis Personae ~ A Book of Names

All titles are available from Amazon

"Leave this chanting and singing and telling of beads. Whom dost thou worship in this lonely dark corner of a temple with doors all shut? Open thine eyes and see thy God is not before thee...Meet him and stand by him in toil and in the sweat of thy brow."

Rabindranath Tagore "Gitanjali" 11

INTRODUCTION

"A Simpler Path" springs from the belief that organised religion, particularly that of Christianity has become over-complicated and burdened by theology and doctrine which actually hinder our spiritual growth.

As a solution to this problem, two alternatives are offered. The first is to be found in the writings of the Fourteenth Century mystic, Dame Julian of Norwich; the second, in the Second Century "Meditations" of Marcus Aurelius. Though springing from different sources, I believe that both these alternatives chart a simpler path to self-enlightenment and may be of some help in achieving that goal.

The Revelations of Divine Love

Dame Julian of Norwich

I used to believe that there was an intellectual and an institutional basis for religion and I suppose that most religions are still shaped by such beliefs. As a result, religion has become inseparable from doctrines and practices which claim to give us access to the divine. Certainly, as a young boy growing up in the Catholic faith I found comfort in its doctrinal and philosophical framework, reinforced by the liturgical practices of the Church, all of which made for a very safe and secure world.

Disenchantment with the theory and the practise of the Christian faith, however, has led many to explore other ways of self-enlightenment. One of the most famous of those seeking an alternative path to truth is Ralph Waldo Emerson (1803 – 1882).

Writing in the Nineteenth Century, the son of a Christian minister, Emerson turned his back on organised religion to follow a philosophy based upon his belief in the divinity of the soul. Echoing Cicero's observation: "Your real self is the spirit inside. Understand that you are God,"[1] Emerson came to champion the view that God is in every man and, indeed, in all creation; an expression of the infinite law which lies within us all:

"I believe that the error of religionists lies in this, that

they do not know the extent or the harmony or the depth

of their moral nature; that they are clinging to little,

positive, verbal, formal versions of the moral law, while

the infinite laws are all unobserved."[2]

This extract, which comes from his "Journal" of 8 September, 1833, forms a prologue to Emerson's life-long advocacy of the spiritual life ~ the life of the soul within us all and throughout the universe.

I have a lot of sympathy with Emerson's train of thought but my own reflections on the limitations of organised religion have led me in a rather different direction.

Looking back over a period of more than sixty years, the Catholic orthodoxy in which I grew up now seems a rather complacent world: over-intellectualised and over-dependent upon externals. In its place and as I reach the age of 80, I now look for understanding in the work of a Fourteenth Century woman, Dame Julian of Norwich.

Neither a scholar nor even a cleric, Dame Julian, in her writing, seems to get closer to a living understanding of the divine than any other writer I have come across.

In May 1373, at the age of thirty and a half, Dame Julian suffered a serious illness and for three days and nights she hovered on the brink of death. At one point her mother, who was nursing her, sent for the curate to administer the last rites. Holding a cross before her face, he urged Julian to take comfort from it. Suddenly, all her pain was taken from her and in a series of sixteen visions, or "shewings", as she called them, she experienced all the sufferings of Christ's Passion.

Julian survived this ordeal and spent the rest of her life, from the safety and security of an anchor-hold adjacent to the small church of Saint Julian in Norwich, in reflecting upon the visions she had experienced. After fifteen years or more she was able to record this experience in *Revelations of Divine Love* ~ the first book written by a woman in English.[3]

Julian's book contains no injunction to follow a particular moral code or to embrace any missionary programme. Neither a preacher nor a prophet, Julian offers us merely a window on the divine. Her message is simple and one which strips Christianity of much of its theological and organisational baggage, leaving us with the simple truth that God loves us all, unconditionally, and seeks nothing more than to be loved in return.

The focus of Julian's book is on the suffering endured by Jesus Christ which draws our attention to a quite different God from that celebrated in ancient Jewish belief and even in much of Christian theology today. In the person of Jesus, God turns out to be not some Old Testament law-giver, or some New Testament missionary telling us how to live our lives; but a servant-king and displaced God: a man of sorrows and one acquainted with grief. As the Anglican theologian, Austin Farrar, once observed: "God did not send us an explanation; he sent us His son."

For Julian, therefore, Christ's sacrifice establishes a new relationship between God and man ~ one that places Him within our sensory being and makes us His true dwelling place. The kingdom of God is within us.

Julian's *Revelations*, with their focus on Christ's suffering and God's love for us all, encourage us to reflect on the theology of Creation and why God became Man.

Julian certainly sees God as Love and the source of all creation. Unfortunately, this is a flawed Creation since the love behind it is freely given and must be freely received. God's love cannot be forced upon us and we are all free to accept or reject it. This freedom of choice is what lies behind our broken universe and our dysfunctional world.[4]

I believe that, in an attempt to repair this situation, God re-entered his Creation in the person of his Son, Jesus Christ, and became man. This re-entry occurred in an historical time and place, against the back ground of a Jewish religion, dating back to around 1000 B.C. and located in the Middle East.

Certain features of the Jewish faith help to explain why God chose the Jews to provide the setting for His inauguration of a new Creation.

From the outset, the Jews identified themselves as the people of Yahweh and their commitment to a single, national God set them apart from other religions. This is made abundantly clear in Deuteronomy, one of the earliest books of the Old Testament, in which the Jews are told: "You have recognised the Lord as your God; you are to conform to His ways… The Lord has recognised you this day as His special Possession." Deuteronomy 26,17-18.

The Jews identified this god as the source of all Creation but recognised that His Creation was marred by human sin and rebellion. They believed, however, that the goal of history was a new Creation through which God's original intention would be fulfilled.

They further believed that God would, at some point in time, intervene in history by sending a saviour, or Messiah, to deliver them from suffering and injustice. In this way the Jewish faith came to provide the necessary framework for God's re-entry into Creation. Without it, Christianity would not have been possible.

Christ, a Jew, is a product and expression of these Jewish beliefs and he clearly saw himself as the fulfilment of the Old Law of Moses, the Prophet and the Psalms, (Luke 24 • 44). In fulfilment of these beliefs, however, the role he assumes is not that of some Master of the Universe but that of a Just Man, bearing the sins of others and going meekly to his death for them. (*Isaiah 53*)

In this way, Christ's birth and death establish an entirely new relationship between God and Man: one built not upon dominance, control and blind obedience but on the unconditional giving and receiving of love ~ a new relationship, foretold in the *Prophecy of Jeremiah* (31.31-34) and one written not on tablets of stone but in our hearts.

Seen in these terms, the love which fills the Universe is extremely vulnerable: an infinitely small, "infinitely gentle, infinitely suffering thing."[5]

Nowhere is this vulnerability more poignantly expressed than in the person of Jesus Christ, through whom God re-enters His Creation, not to rule and control us, but to remind us of the importance of love in our lives. This is very much the theme of *Revelations of Divine Love* and it should lie at the heart of the Christian message, guiding our every thought and action. We have no need of a religion built on rituals and regulations. Love is all we need.

"Thoughts for the Journey", which follow, are largely based on the writings of Dame Julian of Norwich and may be of some help in exploring her vision of the Divine and her simple faith in the power of love.

Reference

1   Cicero "The Dream of Scipio" from "Cicero on the Good Life"

M. Grant Penguin P. 353

2   Sam Torode "Living from the Soul" P. 77

3   David Conduct "All you Need is Love" A Julian of Norwich Handbook

Amazon

4   David Conduct "Mending a Broken Universe" Amazon

5   T.S Eliot "Selected Poems" Faber P.24

Thoughts for the Journey

† A New Covenant with God ~ a Simpler Path

I will make a new covenant with Israel. It will not be

like the covenant I made when I led them out of Egypt. This

covenant which I will make with Israel, I will set within them

and write it on their hearts.

No longer need they teach one another to know the

Lord. All of them, high and low alike, shall know me, says the

Lord, for I will forgive their wrong-doings and remember

their sin no more.

Jeremiah 31 v. 31-34.

† God is Love

God is Love. He who dwells in love is dwelling in God, and God in him. Everyone who loves is a child of God and knows God. The love of which I speak is not our love for God but the love He showed to us in sending His Son as the remedy for our sins. We love God because He loved us first.

St. John's First Epistle 4.7 -20 ' The New English Bible '.

I often desired to know what was Our Lord's meaning and fifteen years after and more I was answered in spiritual understanding, saying this: "What? Would you know your Lord's meaning in this thing? Know it well. Love was his meaning. Who revealed it to you? Love. Why did He reveal it to you? For Love. Hold on to this and you will know more of the same." Thus did I learn that Love is Our Lord's meaning. And I saw surely in this and in everything that our God made us, he loved us and will never cease from loving us. In this love our life is everlasting. In our making we had beginning, but the Love in which he made us was in him from without beginning.

Revelations of Divine Love Cap. 86

The Quantum of Love

He showed me a little thing, the size of a hazelnut in the palm of my hand, and it was as round as a ball. I looked at it with my mind's eye and I thought, 'What can this be?' And answer came: 'It is all that is made.' I marvelled that it could last, for I thought it might have crumbled to nothing, it was so small. And answer came into my mind: 'It lasts and ever shall because God loves it.' And all things have being through the Love of God.

Revelations of Divine Love Cap. 5

✝ Love as Play

*Let love be the one that works. Simply
consent to it. Simply watch and let it be.*

*It is enough to feel moved in love by something,
though you know not what it is.*

*Play some kind of game with God as a
father plays with his child, kissing and
embracing it.*

The Fourteenth Century "Cloud of Unknowing"

† God is a Suffering Christ and a Just Man

I saw the sweet face as it were dry and bloodless, with pale dying and dead pale languor. This was a pitiful change, to see this deep dying. Here I saw a great oneness between Christ and us, to my understanding; for when He was in pain we were in pain and all creatures that might suffer pain, suffered with Him.

Revelations of Divine Love Cap. 16

The servant will appear among us, unregarded as brushwood shoot, as a plant in waterless soil: no beauty, no majesty here to win our hearts, as we gaze upon him. Here is one despised, bowed down with misery; how should we recognise that face? It was our weakness and it was he who carried the weight of it; our miseries and it was he who bore them. For our sins he was wounded and our guilt crushed him down. Strayed sheep, all of us, and God laid on his shoulders our guilt, the guilt of us all. Like sheep led to slaughter, like a lamb that stands dumb while it is shorn: no word from him.

Isaiah 53

A Natural Man

Oh didn't he wear dirty brown hair and a beard

all matted down. Handsome and tanned, just a natural man, with sandals scraping the ground.

* *I remember the time and I still call it mine, when he walked the streets with a few; cracking the seams in conformity's beams with a message so old it was new...*

* *Word got around and folks came to town, to see the love on his face; but he saw the crowds, called them all mobs and sprayed them with chemical faith...*

* *Well they drove him away to the Court-house today, he's charged with unspeakable crimes: Incitement to riot, sedition and treason, assault, all at a time...*

* *At the top of the hill they awaited the kill, as they stood and pretended that he cried; for they knew he would live and say 'Father forgive', but this time he just hung in the sky... Oh didn't he wear dirty brown hair and a beard all matted down. Handsome and tanned, just a natural man, with sandals scraping the ground.*

'Natural Man', a song by Dick Holler, from Dion Di Mucci's
Album, 'Sit Down Old Friend' 1970

† God is Within Us

Our Lord opened my spiritual eyes and showed me my soul in the midst of my heart. I saw it as if it were an endless world, a blessed kingdom and a glorious city.

The noble city in which our Lord Jesus sits is our sensory being in which He is enclosed, and our natural substance is enclosed in Jesus.

Through all eternity Jesus will never vacate the place He takes in our soul, for in our soul is His true dwelling place.

Revelations of Divine Love Cap. 56 and 67

✝ God's Mercy is Infinite

We by sin and wretchedness have in us a wrath and a constant antagonism to peace and to love. And this he often showed in his loving look of care and pity. For the ground of mercy is in love and I could not regard mercy in any other terms than it were all love in love; which is to say, in my view, that mercy is a sweet, gracious working in love, mixed with plentiful pity. Our failing is dreadful, our falling is shameful, and our dying is sorrowful. But yet, in all this, the sweet eye of pity and love never departs from us and the working of mercy never ceases.

Revelations of Divine Love Cap. 48

† God is our Protector

*God wants us to know that he keeps us safe
Through good and ill.*

*Nothing happens by chance but by the
Far-sighted wisdom of God.*

*Constantly and lovingly
God brings all that happens
To its best end.*

*All shall be well and
All manner of thing
Shall be well.*

Revelations of Divine Love Cap. 27

✝ From the Aramaic Version of the Lord's Prayer

You are the song that beautifies all.

You are the force that sustains all life.

You are the fire and birthing glory.

You return all light and sound to the Cosmos.

"Prayers of the Cosmos" Neil Douglas-Klotz.

A CONCLUSION

Substituting the word 'Love' for the 'Word' at the beginning of St. John's Gospel provides us with a new vision of Creation:

Love already was at the beginning of Time;

and Love was with God at the beginning of Time

and it was through Love that all things came into

being. Without Love came nothing that has come

to be ... And Love was made flesh and came to dwell among us

St. John's Gospel 1•1-3 Knox translation.

Seen in these terms Love is the source of Creation and the Universe is the product of its explosive force ~ the singularity of point zero. Let us call this force 'God': the Quantum of love.

Christianity is an attempt to explain the 'why' of this creation and Dame Julian clearly identifies it with God's desire to share his love with us. Unfortunately, this love must be shared freely and we are all free to accept or reject it. Without such freedom of choice Creation would simply be an exercise in self-indulgence on the part of some all-powerful God.

In this sense, the act of Creation represents an abdication and renunciation by God of his infinite power for man is free to accept or reject God's love. In a world of matter God withdraws to allow other things to be. (Simone Weil) The result is that separate wills now exist which may, or may not, return the gift of God's love. The consequence is a broken universe, a world of disorder and disharmony.

In Christian theology, harmony is restored by the sacrifice of God's Son, which opens up the possibility of mankind's reconciliation with God and its return to a world of love, which was the source and purpose of Creation.

Our freedom of choice, however, still remains and this makes Love an extreme paradox: the source of all power and yet helpless to enforce its power on us.

This is clearly reflected in the person of Jesus Christ through whom God re-enters His Creation: not as some Old Testament super-power, but as a displaced God seeking a home in each and every one of us.

The Quantum of Love only finds fulfilment and perfection in infinite sharing ~ in the Lover and the Loved becoming one. This is our true goal and our journey's end: a simple path.

The Meditations of Marcus Aurelius

Edited G. Long

INTRODUCTION

The current popularity of the *Meditations* of Marcus Aurelius is reflected in the huge number of English translations now available. My own favourite is the Victorian text of George Long. This contains a very interesting and well-informed review of the life of Marcus Aurelius, together with a sound appraisal of the Stoic philosophy which lies behind his Meditations.

At the same time, however, Long's prose style is rather dated and may not be to everyone's taste; while his scholarly approach may be off-putting.

My intention in writing about the *Meditations*, therefore, is to identify some of the key thoughts of Marcus Aurelius, as expressed in Long's translation from the Greek, while modifying slightly their prose expression, in the hope that this will create a simple, but elegant, vademecum for the reader's daily use.

Marcus Aurelius

The Making of a Philosopher

Marcus Aurelius was born at Rome in A.D. 121, on the twenty-sixth of April. Following the death of his father, Annius Verus, he became the adopted son of the Emperor Antoninus Pius and in 137 A.D., at the age of sixteen he took the name of Antoninus, as a tribute to his adoptive father. As a result, he is generally named M. Aurelius Antoninus or simply Marcus Antoninus.

He proved to be a dutiful son and as a young man he worked closely with Antoninus Pius in the administration of state affairs. On the latter's death in March 161 A.D. he was appointed Emperor at the age of 39 ~ a position which he shared for a short time with Lucius Verus, another adopted son of Antoninus Pius.

As a young boy, Marcus Aurelius received an excellent education and in Book 1 of his *Meditations* he speaks with great fondness of the support that he received from family, friends and teachers. From the age of 11 he wore the dress of a philosopher, simple and austere, and followed a harsh regime of self-denial which caused him some physical harm. All this was a product of his own serious disposition and the influence of a number of different Stoic philosophers who acted as his teachers. Among them were Marcus Cornelius Fronto, Junius Rusticus and Claudius Maximus, from all of whom he learned "self-government, and not to be led aside by anything; and cheerfulness in all circumstances, as well as in illness." (Book 1•15)

Such teaching shaped the character of the young Marcus Aurelius and ensured that when he assumed the role of Emperor he was well-equipped to handle the heavy responsibility of Imperial office. Much of the responsibility involved protecting the frontiers of the Empire from barbarian incursions, particularly to the north of Italy, by Germanic tribes.

The *Meditations* of Marcus Aurelius, therefore, were certainly not the product of a sedentary scholar's life. They took shape against a background of intense political and military activity and in fact were largely written in the last ten years of his life while on campaign in Lower Pannonia, near what is modern Vienna. There he died on 17 March, 180 A.D. He was 58.

Stoicism

Since the beginning of the First Century B.C. the Roman upper classes had been bi-lingual. Marcus Aurelius, therefore, was fluent in both Latin and Greek. Greek writers and philosophers were numerous in Rome at this time and it was through them that Romans, such as Marcus Aurelius, acquired their philosophy which was overwhelmingly that of Stoicism.

Eschewing the abstract philosophising which distinguished the work of Plato and Aristotle, Greek Stoic philosophy focussed its concern upon morality and how to live the Good Life ~ issues which had an obvious appeal to the practical-minded Roman Citizen.

Stoic philosophy has its origins in the work of Zeno (332-262 B.C.) who lectured in Athens in a down-town area known as the 'Stoa', or covered porchway. His writings and those of his followers, such as Chrysippus (280-207 B.C.), laid the foundations of the philosophy of Stoicism.

Stoic ideas spread to Rome through the expansion of the Roman Republic which led to many Greek philosophers coming to Rome in the Second Century B.C. to lecture, and for many young, upper class Romans to study in Athens. Greek philosophy, of the Stoic kind had strong appeal to the citizens of Rome and this is the sense in which "captive Greece took captive Rome." (Horace)

Cato the Younger (92-46 B.C.) is an early example of this Stoic Greek influence and his suicide in 46 B.C. is an expression of resistance to Caesar's tyranny which clearly reflects this influence. The same is true of Seneca the Younger (4 B.C. – 65 A.D.), whose writings and his own death from suicide are a clear expression of Stoic philosophy.

Of less exalted background than Cato or Seneca, however, were Musonius Rufus (3-100 A.D.) and the Greek slave, Epictetus (55-135 A.D.) whose work on Stoic philosophy (via Arrian's 'Discourses of Epictetus', the 'Enchiridion') was particularly influential on the young Marcus Aurelius.

Central to the Stoic philosophy which shaped Aurelius' thoughts and outlook on life is the belief that, in spite of all appearances to the contrary, the Universe is wisely ordered and that everyone is a part of it and must conform to it. All mankind are our brethren and we must love and cherish them and try to make them better ~ even those who would do us harm.

According to this philosophy, nothing is evil that is according to Nature. Reason, or 'Logos' pervades all substance and through all time administers the Universe. Nature is an everlasting continuity for "Everything that exists is, in a manner, the seed of that which will be." (Book 4 • 36)

Everything is in some way related to and connected to every other thing; and so the notion of evil as being in the Universe of things is a contradiction. The evil which is manifestly present in the world is not the product of some malign force. Men do wrong, but do so involuntarily so that there is no evil in anything which is not in our power to correct. What wrong we suffer from another, therefore, is 'his' evil, not ours. Evil is not part of the constitution of things: if it were, then evil would no longer be evil but be good.

The ethical part of the Stoic philosophy of Marcus Aurelius follows from these general principles and the end of his philosophy is to live in conformity to Nature, both our own Nature and the Nature of the Universe.

We must, therefore, not retire into solitude, nor cut ourselves off from our fellow man. We must engage with life and play our part in the great whole. All men are our brothers. We cannot be really harmed by them for no act

of theirs can make 'us' bad and so we must not hate them
or be angry with them. We are made for co-operation.

The Thoughts of Marcus Aurelius

~ A Vademecum ~

The Social Contract

* Begin the morning by saying to yourself: I shall meet with the busybody, the ungrateful, arrogant, envious, deceitful, unsocial. But I that have seen the nature of the good, that it is beautiful and of the bad, that it is ugly, can neither be injured by any of them, for no man can fix on me what is ugly, nor can I be angry with my fellow-man, nor hate him. For we are made for co-operation like feet, like hands, like eyelids, like the rows of the upper and lower teeth. To act against one another then is contrary to Nature; and it is acting against one another to be vexed and turn away.* Book 2 • 1

* *In the morning when you rise unwillingly, let this thought be present: I am rising to the work of a human being. Why then am I dissatisfied if I am going to do the things for which I exist and for which I was brought into the world? Are you unwilling to do the work of a human being?* Book 5 • 1

* *Men exist for the sake of one another.* Book 8 • 59

* *Love of one's neighbour is the property of the rational soul.* Book 11 •1

* *Have I done something for the general interest? Well then, I have my reward. Let this always be present in your mind and never stop from doing good.* Book 11 • 4

Mind over Matter

Things do not touch the soul for they are external to it. Our worries and anxiety come only from opinion, which lies within us. Book 4 • 3.

Things themselves do not touch the soul, nor can they turn or move the soul; for the soul turns and moves itself alone. Book 5 • 19

Look within. Let neither the peculiar quality of anything nor its value escape you. Book 6 • 3

No man can rob us of our free will. Book 11 • 36

Tranquillity is nothing else than the good ordering of the mind. It is within your power, whenever you choose, to retire into yourself. Book 4 • 3

The Problem of Evil

*   *The substance of the Universe is obedient and compliant. The Reason or Logos which governs it has in itself no cause for doing evil, for it has no malice, nor does it do evil to anything, nor is anything harmed by it. All things are made and perfected according to this Reason.* Book 6 • 1

*   *Are you discontented with the badness of mankind? Recall to your mind that rational animals exist for one another, and that men do wrong involuntarily.* Book 4 • 3

*   *Generally, wickedness does no harm at all to the Universe; and particularly, the wickedness of one man does no harm to another. It is only harmful to him who has it in his power to be released from it, as soon as he shall choose.* Book 8 • 55

* *What wrong we suffer from another is his evil, not ours. He who does wrong does wrong against himself, because 'he' makes himself bad.* Book 9 • 4

* *If it is not right do not do it; if it is not true do not say it.* Book 12 • 17

The Nature of the Universe

* *The Universe loves nothing so much as to change the things that are and to make new things like them. For everything that exists is, in a manner, the seed of that which will be.* Book 4 • 36

* *Constantly regard the Universe as one living being.* Book 4 • 30

* *Frequently consider the connection of all things in the Universe and their relation to one another. For, in a manner, all things are implicated with one another.* Book 6 • 38

* *The Universe is transformation: life is opinion.* Book 4 • 3

* *Reverence that which is best in the Universe and, in like manner, also reverence that which is best within yourself.* Book 5 • 21

The Nature of Time

*   *All things from eternity are of like forms and come round in a circle. It makes no difference whether a man shall see the same things during a hundred years or two hundred, or an infinite time. The longest liver and he who dies soonest lose just the same. For the present is the only thing of which a man can be deprived. Book 2 • 14*

*   *Do not act as if you were going to live ten thousand years. Death hangs over you. While you live, while it is in your power, be good.* Book 4 • 17

*   *All things soon pass away and become a mere tale and complete oblivion soon buries them.* Book 4 • 33

*   *Consider that before long you will be nobody and nowhere; nor will any of the things which exist, which now you see, nor any of those who are now living. For all things are formed by Nature to change and to perish in order that other things may exist.* Book 12 • 21

Time is like a river, made up of events which happen and a violent stream. As one thing is seen, it is carried away and another comes in its place. Book 4 • 43

Our Spiritual Identity

To those who ask me: 'Where have you seen the Gods, or how do you comprehend that they exist and so worship them?' I answer: neither have I seen my own soul and yet I honour it. Book 12 • 28

About what am I now employing my own soul? On every occasion I must ask myself this question. Book 5 • 11

'You are a little soul bearing about a corpse,' as Epictetus used to say. Book 4 • 41

"The Meditations" of Marcus Aurelius clearly spring from a different source than that of Dame Julian of Norwich but, in their simplicity and their clarity; in their focus on the social contract which links us all; and in their faith in a benign universe, free from the power of evil, they point in much the same direction.

Taken together, the Love and Reason explored by Dame Julian and by Marcus Aurelius chart a simpler path to self-fulfilment. Enjoy the journey.

Ave atque Vale

POST SCRIPT

No one has ever seen God and yet many religions seem to be based upon a belief in both the physical and the spiritual presence of God. Kings and priests alike share this belief and the result has been the creation over time of religions whose doctrines and practices claim to give us access to the divine. But do they? Why is religion so complicated and why does God's message seem to vary from person to person and from one religion to another? As Deepak Chopra has observed: "The messages keep coming but God keeps showing different faces." (.Deepak Chopra "God " 1)

I suppose that the answer lies in the symbiotic relationship between the spiritual and the secular which has shaped the history of mankind. The human mind has always had a capacity for higher understanding of reality, as reflected, for example, in the Palaeolithic cave art of Lascaux. Unfortunately, mankind's search for meaning in life has always been exploited by secular and religious authority to provide a basis for social behaviour and justification for the existence of both Church and State. Rarely in history has mankind's desire for meaning been allowed free expression and certainly in the Christian Middle Ages the individual's pursuit of inner truth was often defined as heresy and ruthlessly suppressed.

As Friedrich Heer observes in his study of the medieval world, even a Dominican mystic like Meister Eckhart (1260 – 1327) could be condemned by a Pope (John XX11) for trying to defend the right of an individual to experience the divine within his own soul: " The mystic's theme,"Heer says, "is that men should look for the kingdom of God within themselves. All the splendour of heaven and earth is to be found in the soul, the hiding place of God. The inmost citadel of the soul will stand where castles and churches have failed to give shelter. Eckhart himself dwells much on this tiny inner citadel in the heart. Within it burns the flame of Godhead, light, fire, strength, the spark of the soul. ' Cherish this flame,'says Eckhart, 'and let God awake within you.'" (F. Heer " The Medieval World" 310)

Sadly, the individual's pursuit of such inner vision has found little support in either Judaism, Christianity or Islam and the result has been to leave mankind with little room for a truly personal experience of the divine.

From a Christian point of view, of course, the solution is quite simple and is to be found in St.John's First Epistle where the Apostle of Love, whom Jesus loved most dearly , boldly declares, "No one has ever seen God but if we love one another then God lives within us and His love is perfected in us." (John First Epistle 4 , 12 Knox)

As I have already observed, this thought allows us to substitute the word, 'Love ' for the 'Word' at the beginning of St. John's Gospel to provide a new version of Creation, for " without Love came nothing that has come to be." (John 1-3 Knox)

Seen in these terms, Love is the source of all Creation and this finds an echo in the Aramaic version of the Lord's Prayer, as translated by Neil Douglas-Klotz in his Prayers of the Cosmos: " Father and Mother of the Cosmos, creator of all that is ; source of sound and radiant light that shines within us all; your name can move all things if we tune out hearts to its tone; you are the song that beautifies all; you are the force that sustains all life. You are the fire and the birthing glory. You restore all light and sound to the Cosmos".

This, from the original, poetic version of the Lord's Prayer, sets it apart from the prosaic, logical version derived from the Ancient Greek translation of the New Testament and creates quite a different image of God, one with no bodily presence and no particular gender. As such, it supports St.John's assertion that, " No one has ever seen God" and speaks to the importance of love in our lives. And this is surely reflected in Christ's own response to the disciples of John the Baptist, seeking proof of his Divinity:- "Tell John what you have seen and heard: the blind see, the lame walk, the lepers are cleansed, the deaf hear,the dead rise again and the poor have the Gospel preached unto them." (Matt. 11. 12) Clearly, for Christ compassion for others took precedence over formal instruction.

In the monotheistic religions of Judaism, Christianity and Islam, however, this simple view of the divine has become lost, replaced by systems of rules and rituals, enshrined in written form, which have had the effect of turning their respective Churches into teaching institutions and instruments of control.

As long ago as the time of Jeremiah, however,(650-570BC)there have been those who have called for a simpler path and, as we have seen, for Jeremiah this was to be found in a New Covenant with God, one not set in tablets of stone but written in people's hearts, without the need for elaborate instruction.(Jeremiah 31,31-34)

As I hope this book makes clear, in the Christian faith my own favourite advocate of a simpler path is Dame Julian of Norwich who sees Jesus Christ as the means through which God re-enters His Creation, not to rule and control us but to remind us of the importance of Love in our lives: a Love which is infinitely small, as reflected in her mystical experience of the hazelnut, the Quantum of Love, which is recalled on page 12.

There are echoes in this experience of the Chinese mystic, Lao-Tzu, who lived nearly 2000 years before Dame Julian and who saw Creation in terms of the Tao:

> 'There is a thing inherent and natural
>
> Which existed before heaven and earth.
>
> Motionless and fathomless,
>
> It stands alone and never changes.
>
> It pervades everything and is illimitable,

> It may be regarded as the source of the Universe
>
> I call it Tao and name it as Supreme
>
> From the Tao the infinite complexity of the Cosmos Has taken shape.'
>
> From Lao-Tzu's "Tao-Te-Ching"

Remarkably, such views of the divine find some support in theoretical physics and quantum mechanics where the Big Bang of Lemaitre's primordial atom and the infinite complexity of photons and electrons give rise to speculation that science is getting close to identifying the 'God ' particle responsible for the creation of the Universe.

Seen from this point of view the Universe, which we know began some 13.8 billion years ago, is the product of a burst of high-explosive energy. Call it God, the Tao, or the First Particle, this Quantum of Love is the source of all Creation and God and Science meet in its infinite smallness.

Like the Tao and the electron particle, this Love is in everyone, in everything, in every place, at every time. We know this partly through the study of quantum mechanics but mainly through the exercise of Love in our lives.

We don't need the rules, ritual and dogma associated with organised religion and Therese of Lisieux sums it all up for us in the following way:

' Jesus has no need of books or teachers to instruct souls. He teaches without the noise of words.Never have I heard him speak but I feel that he is within me at each moment, guiding and inspiring what I must say and do.'(Autobiography).This is a view shared perhaps by St.Paul when he admits, 'The letter kills but the spirit restores to life.'(Corinthians 2,3-6)

All we need ,then,is Love and to love our neighbour we do not have to know calculus or the Ten Commandments. The truth is simple and self- evident and perhaps best expressed by Jacob Bronowski when, in his famous television series, 'The Ascent of Man ',while standing outside the extermination camp of Auschwitz, in the marshy ground where the ashes of cremated Jews were scattered and stretching out his hands in the stagnant water, he observed, 'We have to cure ourselves of the itch for absolute knowledge and power... we have to touch people.'Or,as Marcus Aurelius puts it: 'We exist for the sake of one another.'

******** ******** ******

Finally,what better critique of the part played by organised religion in people's lives can be found than that provided by Robert Burton in his 'Anatomy of Melancholy' published in 1621?

For an Oxford cleric, Burton shows surprisingly little sympathy for organised religion and indeed identifies it as a most notable symptom and source of melancholy. Superstition, heresy and schism, he claims, have caused more madness, more harm and more anxiety to mankind than wars, plagues famines and all the rest.

He identifies priests as a major cause of the mental confusion from which we suffer, ' for they domineer over princes and statesmen themselves.What have they not made the common people believe? What devices, traditions, ceremonies, have they not invented in all ages to keep men in obedience, to enrich themselves?'

And, of course, they are assisted in their work by the universal prevalence of human gullibility. 'For the common people are as a flock of sheep, a rude, illiterate rout, void many times of common sense, a mere beast and will go wherever they are led.' Fear of the unknown reinforces this gullibility for as Petronius observes, 'Fear first created Gods in the world'and the fear of divine, supreme power enables priests and their like to keep people in obedience and make them do their duties- 'they play upon their consciences.'

Among the symptoms of religious melancholy the most prominent is an extraordinary love and affection for members of the same sect, combined with an inordinate hatred for all those who are not members. As Montanus observes, 'no greater concord, no greater discord than that which proceeds from religion.'

Christianity, Judaism and Islam, Burton tells us, are all distinguished by this obsessive regard for the rightness of their beliefs:

> 'In a word, this is common to all Superstition, there is nothing so mad and so absurd, so ridiculous, impossible, incredible, which they will not believe and diligently perform, as much as in them lies; nothing so monstrous to conceive, or intolerable to put into practise, so cruel to suffer, which they will not willingly undertake. So powerful a thing is Superstition.' And, of course, this is even more true of pagan religions: 'Of those ridiculous, there can be no better testimony than the multitude of their gods, those absurd names, actions, offices they put upon them, their feasts, holy days, sacrifices, adorations and the like.'

Although reserving his harshest criticism for the Roman Catholic Church, Burton sees both Judaism and Islam as prime examples of the madness of religion and his censure of them would certainly make him the target of a 'fatwah' if expressed in this form today. To his credit, however, Burton is equally critical of the Puritan fundamentalism which threatened the Anglican Church of his day, describing it as 'a devil which will never suffer the Church to be quiet or at rest... They will admit of no holidays or honest recreations, any interpretations of Scripture, but such as their own phantastical spirits dictate.'

'What greater madness can there be', Burton asks, 'than for a man to take upon him to be a God, as some do? They are certainly far gone with melancholy, if not quite mad?'

(All quotations are from the Third Partition on the subject of Religious Melancholy).

***** ***** ***** *****

Bibliography

- David Conduct 'All You Need is Love ' A Julian of Norwich Handbook. Amazon
- Serenus de Cressy, author of the 1670 translation of 'Revelations of Divine Love shewed to a Devout Servant of God called Mother Juliana.' The main source of my quotations and still the best version of the text.
- 'Revelations of Divine Love ', a beautiful hardback version of this book published by the Folio Society.
- Sam Torode 'Living from the Soul.'
- George Long 'The Meditations of Marcus Aurelius.'
- 'Robert Burton's The Anatomy of Melancholy -An Abridged Version.' David Conduct. Amazon and IngramSpark.

www.ingramcontent.com/pod-product-compliance
Lightning Source LLC
Chambersburg PA
CBHW050205130526
44591CB00034B/2144